HOW IT'S MADE
HANUKKAH MENORAH

by Allison Ofanansky • Photographs by Eliyahu Alpern

Happy Hanukkah!
love,
Grammy + Papa

We would like to thank the many people who shared their time and knowledge with us:

Gabriel Bass, Bass Synagogue Furniture, Moshav Mata, Israel, www.basssynagoguefurniture.com
David Goldhagen, Goldhagen Studios, Hayesville, NC, www.goldhagenartglass.com
Efim Levin, Tzfat, Israel, www.efimlevin.com
Hasmonian Village, Shilat, Israel, www.hasmonian.co.il/GuidedTour.html
Migdal Olive Press, Migdal, Israel
Sheva Chaya Servetter, Sheva Chaya Gallery, Tzfat, Israel, www.shevachaya.com
Sheva Deganim Bakery, Tzfat, Israel
Kathleeen Wasserman, Quilted Art Glass, Tzfat, Israel, www.QuiltedArtGlass.com
Yossi, Nerot Beresheet, Hadera, Israel
100% Pure Beeswax Candles, Big Dipper Wax Works, Seattle, WA, www.bigdipperwaxworks.com
Emmanuel Gallery of Fine Art in Tzfat, Israel, http://tzfatart.com/
The publisher wishes to credit the following sources of additional photographs and illustrations:
Adobe Stock: Moon phases on page 4, wooden plank on page 7, magnifying glass on pages 10 and 20, brass borders on pages 10–11,
glass borders on pages 12–13, wood borders on pages 14–15, crafting supplies on page 17, honeycomb background on page 19, plate of latkes on page 24,
dreidels, gift boxes, and gelt on page 28, colorful beeswax candles, wooden boards, olives, honeycomb, and clay ball on page 29
Shutterstock/Tercer Ojo Photography: Grandmother and child on page 31
National Photo Collection of Israel, Photography Department Government Press Office: Family on page 4
Wikimedia Commons: Grandfather and child on page 30
U.S. Air Force photo/Airman 1st Class Nesha Humes: Menorah in Washington, DC, on page 30

Apples & Honey Press
An imprint of Behrman House
Millburn, New Jersey 07041
www.applesandhoneypress.com

Text copyright © 2018 by Allison Ofanansky
Photographs copyright © 2018 by Eliyahu Alpern, except as otherwise noted
ISBN 978-1-68115-534-0

Design by the Virtual Paintbrush · Edited by Amanda Cohen

Library of Congress Cataloging-in-Publication Data

Names: Ofanansky, Allison, author. | Alpern, Eliyahu, photographer.
Title: How it's made : Hanukkah menorah / by Allison Ofanansky ; photographs
    by Eliyahu Alpern.
Description: Millburn, New Jersey : Apples & Honey Press, [2018] |
    Audience: Ages 4–7.
Identifiers: LCCN 2017034784 | ISBN 9781681155340
Subjects: LCSH: Menorah--Design and construction--History--Juvenile literature.
Classification: LCC BM657.M35 O33 2018 | DDC 296.4/61--dc23 LC record available
    at https://lccn.loc.gov/2017034784

Printed in China · 9 8 7 6 5 4 3 2 1

FOR OVER

two thousand years, the Jewish people have celebrated Hanukkah.

Families and friends gather around the menorah to kindle its lights, recite the blessings, and sing traditional songs.

Did you ever wonder HOW a menorah is made?

Choosing the materials

Sketching the design

Crafting the menorah

Attaching the holders

Lighting the menorah

Let's find out . . .

But first . . . what is Hanukkah?

Hanukkah, חֲנוּכָּה in Hebrew, is a Jewish holiday that lasts eight days. It commemorates the restoration of the Temple in Jerusalem after the Maccabees' victory against the Greek empire.

Also known as the Festival of Lights, Hanukkah falls at the darkest time of year. We celebrate it in early winter, when the nights are long and the moon is a thin crescent or invisible, during the Hebrew months of Kislev and Tevet.

Kislev   Tevet

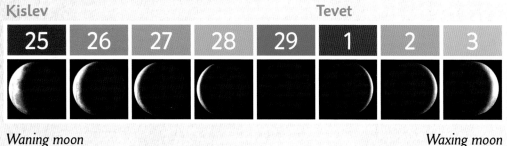

| 25 | 26 | 27 | 28 | 29 | 1 | 2 | 3 |

Waning moon   *Waxing moon*

The word *Hanukkah* means "dedication"

What is a Hanukkah menorah?

The menorah we light on Hanukkah (also called a *hanukkiyah*) holds eight candles or oil cups arranged in a line, plus an extra one, set apart from the others, called the *shamash*.

We light the menorah to celebrate the miracle of the first Hanukkah. Tradition tells us that when the ancient Temple Menorah was lit, a single day's worth of olive oil burned for eight days and nights.

Number of lights in a Hanukkah menorah

9

Sketch of design

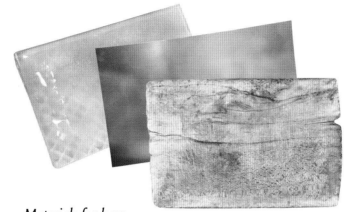

Materials for base

Wicks

What do we need for a Hanukkah menorah?

Oil

Holders for candles or oil

A flame

Candles

Hanukkah Menorahs

There are many types of menorahs. Some are antiques, passed down through a family for generations. Others are bought or made new each year.

Menorahs come in many sizes. Most are small and can be carried easily. Some are taller than a person!

Number of branches on the Temple Menorah

7

Artisans make them in different creative styles and out of various materials.

Making a Brass Menorah

Efim Levin starts by sketching the menorah he wants to make.

He cuts metal for the base . . .

. . . and makes places for the candles to sit.

Take a closer look

Polishing a brass decoration

"In my menorahs I use imagery from North Africa, Europe, Jerusalem—it brings the whole Jewish world together."

—Efim Levin, *artist*

He carves intricate designs in sheets of yellow, white, and red brass . . .

. . . and attaches all the pieces together.

Can you see details from the sketch in the final menorah?

Making a Glass Menorah

Kathleen Wasserman makes fused glass menorahs.

She uses a blowtorch to bend glass threads.

She cuts bits of colored glass . . .

. . . and arranges the pieces on a clear glass background. A sprinkle of glass dust completes this flowery design.

In a hot kiln, the pieces of glass fuse together.

With a wet table saw, she trims off the extra glass.

Last, she glues nine glass candleholders on top.

"Glass menorahs capture and reflect the sparkle of the flames."

–Kathleen Wasserman, *artist*

Making a Wooden Menorah

Gabriel Bass designs revolving menorahs with movable arms.

He measures and sketches a menorah on a piece of wood . . .

. . . cuts it out, and sands the edges smooth.

With hammer, chisel, and knives, he carves and shapes the menorah's arms.

"A menorah should make people—especially kids—excited to share in the custom and hear the story behind it."

—Gabriel Bass, *artist*

He makes blown-glass candle-holders attached to metal rods that screw into the menorah's arms.

He drills a hole through the arms and threads them onto a metal rod, so they can rotate.

A finished menorah has arms that can rotate into different positions.

15

Making Your Own Menorah

Kids can make beautiful Hanukkah menorahs.

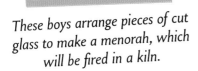

These boys arrange pieces of cut glass to make a menorah, which will be fired in a kiln.

Gluing on acorn caps as candleholders.

Making a clay menorah.

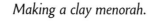

Seashells are being used as candleholders.

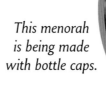

This menorah is being made with bottle caps.

Do It Yourself

Tips for making
your own menorah

- Use natural or recycled materials.

- Avoid materials that will melt or catch fire.

- Secure the candleholders so they won't tip over.

- Make a special place for the *shamash*—it can be above, below, in front of, or behind the other eight candleholders.

- Be creative!

Remember: never leave a menorah
with lit candles unattended.

What would
YOU
like to use to
make a Hanukkah
menorah?

Making Candles

The menorah can be lit with either candles or olive oil.

All candles need wicks—braided strings of cotton or other absorbent material. The wick slowly draws the wax or oil up toward the flame.

Beeswax or paraffin candles are hand dipped or made in a factory.

Over **5,000** years ago people began making candles with wicks

Candlemaker Yossi dips a wick into melted wax, lets the wax cool for a moment, then dips it again and again until the candle is thick enough.

In this factory, workers dip many candles at once.

Make a candle!

An easy way to make a candle is to roll a sheet of beeswax around a wick.

19

Making Olive Oil

Because the Menorah in the ancient Temple burned olive oil, some people enjoy lighting their Hanukkah menorahs with olive oil.

Harvesters collect ripe olives.

Olive oil comes from the fruit of the olive tree.

"On Hanukkah we also celebrate the miracle that such a wonderful thing as olive oil exists!"

—Marc Ben Shabbat, *olive harvester*

Take a closer look

Squeezing oil out of olives

At the oil press, giant stone wheels grind the olives.

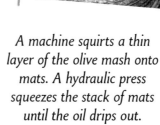

A machine squirts a thin layer of the olive mash onto mats. A hydraulic press squeezes the stack of mats until the oil drips out.

In the days before machines, people or animals moved the heavy olive-crushing stones. These kids find out what hard work that is at an archaeological park in Israel.

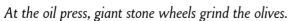

The freshly pressed olive oil pours into a tank.

Lighting the Menorah: One for Each Night

We light the Hanukkah menorah after sunset. First we light the *shamash* and use it to light all the other candles. On the first night, the 25th of Kislev, we light one candle. Each following night, another candle is added from right to left, until the last night when all eight are lit.

44 candles are kindled in a Hanukkah menorah during the festival

Blessings and Songs

Each night after lighting the *shamash* and before kindling the other lights, we say two blessings. On the first night, an additional blessing is said.

We light the candles from left to right.

There are many Hanukkah songs to sing while the candles burn.

סדר הדלקת נרות חנוכה

בָּרוּךְ אַתָּה יְיָ אֱלֹהֵינוּ מֶלֶךְ הָעוֹלָם אֲשֶׁר קִדְּשָׁנוּ בְּמִצְוֹתָיו וְצִוָּנוּ לְהַדְלִיק נֵר שֶׁל חֲנֻכָּה:

בָּרוּךְ אַתָּה יְיָ אֱלֹהֵינוּ מֶלֶךְ הָעוֹלָם שֶׁעָשָׂה נִסִּים לַאֲבוֹתֵינוּ בַּיָּמִים הָהֵם בַּזְּמַן הַזֶּה:

On the first night only:

בָּרוּךְ אַתָּה יְיָ אֱלֹהֵינוּ מֶלֶךְ הָעוֹלָם שֶׁהֶחֱיָנוּ וְקִיְּמָנוּ וְהִגִּיעָנוּ לַזְּמַן הַזֶּה:

What is **YOUR** favorite Hanukkah song?

Do It Yourself

Make Potato Latkes

Another fun way to celebrate Hanukkah is to eat foods fried in oil. Potato latkes are a popular Hanukkah meal.

Ingredients

- 2 pounds raw potatoes
- 1 onion, minced
- 2 eggs, beaten
- 2 tablespoons flour
- ½ teaspoon salt
- olive oil or vegetable oil

Instructions

1. Peel and grate potatoes.
2. Squeeze out as much water as you can.
3. Mix with eggs, flour, salt, and onion.
4. Shape into patties.
5. Heat oil in frying pan. Remember! The oil is hot— always have an adult supervise frying the latkes.
6. Fry until crispy brown on one side.
7. Flip using spatula and fry the second side.
8. Serve with applesauce and/or sour cream.

In Israel, a favorite Hanukkah treat is a donut called a *sufganiah*. The name comes from the Hebrew root "to absorb," because the dough absorbs so much oil!

This bakery makes **2,000** donuts every day of Hanukkah

The baker drops balls of raw dough into a vat of hot oil.

When one side is done, he flips them over.

A bakery worker squeezes jelly into each sufganiah.

I Have a Little Dreidel, I Made It Out of Clay

During Hanukkah it is popular to play a game with a special spinning top called a *dreidel* in Yiddish or a *s'vivon* in Hebrew.

Ceramic artist Talia Ben Shabbat teaches children how to make a dreidel.

First, they form the four-sided body out of a ball of clay.

They cut away the bottom four corners . . .

. . . and smooth it into a point.

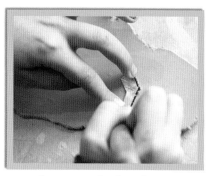

They trace the four letters onto a flat piece of clay . . .

. . . cut them out . . .

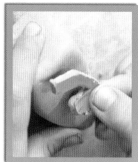

and stick them to the dreidel.

A handle is attached to the top.

The dreidels are fired, then decorated with glaze.

A second firing . . . and the dreidels are ready!

A Great Miracle Happened There

On each side of the dreidel is a Hebrew letter.

The letters stand for the phrase "a great miracle happened there."

נ *Nun* (*nes*—miracle)

ג *Gimmel* (*gadol*—great)

ה *Hay* (*hayah*—happened)

ש *Shin* (*sham*—there)

Dreidels made in Israel substitute

פ *Pay* (*po*—here)

so it reads: "A great miracle happened here."

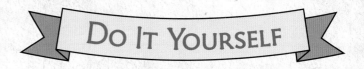

DO IT YOURSELF

Make a Cardboard Dreidel

1. Trace a circle onto thin cardboard.
2. Divide it into four quarters.
3. On each quarter write one of the four letters.
4. Decorate with crayons, stickers, or paint.
5. Cut a wooden skewer to 3 inches long.
6. Push through the center of the circle.
7. Secure with tape.

Gifts and Gelt

There is a tradition of giving children *gelt* (money) or gifts on Hanukkah. Gold-wrapped chocolate coins are eaten and used for playing dreidel.

How to play dreidel with gelt

Before every spin, each player puts one coin into the center of the circle.

Take turns spinning the dreidel. The letter facing up when it falls tells you what to do:

נ — *Nun:* don't take or give any *gelt* coins
ג — *Gimmel:* take all the *gelt* from the center
ה — *Hay:* take half the *gelt*
ש — *Shin:* put one *gelt* coin in the center

Can you match each Hanukkah object with what it's made from?

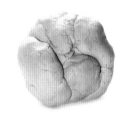

Proclaiming the Miracle

An important part of the tradition is "proclaiming the miracle" by lighting the menorah in a place where the lights can be seen, in a window or on the street.

In Israel, some people light their menorahs in glass boxes outside their houses.

Public menorah lightings in Washington, D.C. (above) and Tzfat (right).

"One for each night
They shed a sweet light
To remind us of days long ago."
—Hanukkah song

Hanukkah connects us to our Jewish roots and history

Lighting the menorah is a symbolic way to celebrate our freedom to observe traditions, to remember a miracle, and to bring light to dark times.

Hanukkah Word Search

H	L	O	M	F	T
C	A	N	D	L	E
W	I	C	K	A	Z
F	B	V	A	M	R
O	I	L	P	E	S
L	I	G	H	T	M

Can you find the five hidden words?

OIL

CANDLE

LIGHT

WICK

FLAME

The Hanukkah Blessings

Each night of the holiday begins with the candle lighting ritual. On the first night, we place a single candle in the holder on the far right of the Hanukkah menorah and light it using the *shamash*, or "helper" candle. We let both candles burn down.

Each successive night, we add another candle, placing the candles from right to left but lighting them with the *shamash* from left to right. On the eighth night, all eight candles plus the *shamash* burn brightly.

We light the candles *after* we say the blessings:

בָּרוּךְ אַתָּה, יְיָ אֱלֹהֵינוּ, מֶלֶךְ הָעוֹלָם, אֲשֶׁר קִדְּשָׁנוּ בְּמִצְוֹתָיו וְצִוָּנוּ לְהַדְלִיק נֵר שֶׁל חֲנֻכָּה.

Baruch Atah, Adonai Eloheinu, Melech ha'olam, asher kid'shanu b'mitzvotav v'tzivanu l'hadlik neir shel Hanukkah.

Praised are You, Adonai our God, Ruler of the world, who makes us holy with commandments and commands us to light the Hanukkah candles.

בָּרוּךְ אַתָּה, יְיָ אֱלֹהֵינוּ, מֶלֶךְ הָעוֹלָם, שֶׁעָשָׂה נִסִּים לַאֲבוֹתֵינוּ בַּיָּמִים הָהֵם, בַּזְּמַן הַזֶּה.

Baruch Atah, Adonai Eloheinu, Melech ha'olam, she'asah nisim la'avoteinu bayamim hahem, bazman hazeh.

Praised are You, Adonai our God, Ruler of the world, who made miracles for our ancestors long ago, at this season.

On the first night, we also say the *Shehecheyanu* blessing:

בָּרוּךְ אַתָּה, יְיָ אֱלֹהֵינוּ, מֶלֶךְ הָעוֹלָם, שֶׁהֶחֱיָנוּ, וְקִיְּמָנוּ, וְהִגִּיעָנוּ לַזְּמַן הַזֶּה.

Baruch Atah, Adonai Eloheinu, Melech ha'olam, shehecheyanu, v'kiy'manu, v'higi'anu lazman hazeh.

Praised are You, Adonai our God, Ruler of the world, who has given us life, sustained us, and enabled us to reach this time.
